B·I·B·L·E W·O·R·L·D

WHERE THE WORLD BEGAN
The Lands of the Bible

To my wife, Helen

Published by
Lion Publishing plc
Sandy Lane West, Oxford, England
ISBN 0 7459 2177 9
Albatross Books Pty Ltd
PO Box 320, Sutherland, NSW 2232, Australia
ISBN 0 7324 0547 5

First edition 1995

10 9 8 7 6 5 4 3 2 1 0

Contributors to this volume
Nigel Hepper, formerly Principal Scientific Officer and Assistant Keeper
of the Herbarium at the Royal Botanic Garden, Kew, introduces the lands
of the Bible.

Alan Millard, Rankin Professor of Hebrew and Ancient Semitic
Languages at Liverpool University, is the consultant for the illustrations
in this book, and all the books in the series.

Acknowledgments
All photographs are copyright © Lion Publishing, except the following:
David Alexander: 17 (right)
J.C.Allen: 2
Nigel Hepper: 3 (all), 5, 6 (left and far right), 7 (left and near right),
8 (above left, right), 10 (all), 12 (above left), 13 (left), 14, 16 (below left,
right), 17 (left), 20
Clifford Shirley: 11 (right)
Zefa: 12 (below right), 19 (right)

The following Lion Publishing photographs appear by courtesy of:
Hai Bar Nature Reserve: 6 (right)
Haifa Maritime Museum: 19 (left)

Illustrations, copyright © Lion Publishing, by:
Chris Molan: 1, 2, 3, 4, 5, 6, 7, 8, 9, 10, 11, 12, 13, 14, 15, 16, 17, 18,
19, 20
Jeffrey Burn: 11 (right), 15 (above)

Maps, copyright © Lion Publishing, by:
Oxford Illustrators Ltd.: 1, 2, 3, 4, 5, 6, 7, 8, 9, 12, 13, 14, 17, 18, 19, 20

Bible quotations are taken from the Good News Bible, copyright ©
American Bible Society, New York, 1966, 1971 and 4th edition 1976,
published by the Bible Societies/HarperCollins, with permission.

Story text is based on material from *The Lion Children's Bible*, by Pat
Alexander

A catalogue record for this book is available
from the British Library

Printed and bound in Malaysia

B·I·B·L·E W·O·R·L·D

WHERE THE WORLD BEGAN

THE LANDS OF THE BIBLE

Nigel Hepper

A LION BOOK

Contents

page 2

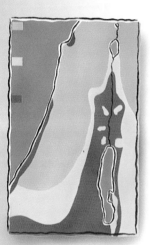

page 5

page 3

page 4

page 6

page 19

page 15

page 3

page 13

1 Lands of the Bible

On the eastern shore of the Mediterranean Sea are two countries known today as Israel and Palestine. They are at the heart of the region where, long ago, people called the Israelites made their home. The stories in the Bible tell their history, and it was here that many of the most dramatic events of the Bible took place.

In Old Testament times, the land was often referred to as Canaan. By New Testament times, the area near the capital city of Jerusalem was a province of the Roman Empire known as Judea.

The 'fertile crescent'

The eastern part of the area shown on this map is known as the Middle East. It is a hot, dry region, and much of it is desert. However, a large area of good land can be found, curving from the Persian Gulf round to the Nile Valley. This is known as the 'fertile crescent'. Much of the action of the Old Testament takes place in this region. There were great empires in the northern area, which today is mainly Iraq. To the south lay another great civilization: Egypt.

The lands of the Mediterranean

Along the northern coast of the Mediterranean Sea are three important areas of land. They are known today as Italy, Greece and Turkey. Invading armies swept into Canaan from these lands at different times in Bible history. In New Testament times, these were among the countries to which the first followers of Jesus took the message of Christianity.

▼ **Where in the world**
The lands of the Bible extend from the Mediterranean Sea to the Persian Gulf. Notice where they belong on the world map.

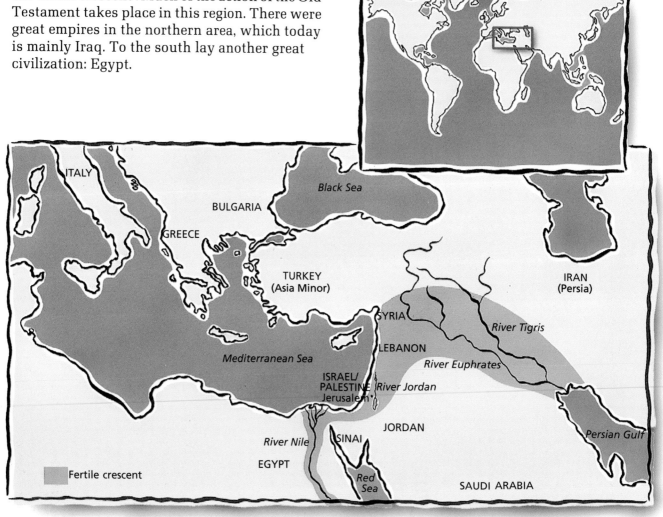

The Holy Land

The name of the land where the Israelites made their home has changed several times. The boundaries of the land have also changed as different peoples have gained control of it. However, nothing can change the fact that two important religions—Judaism and Christianity—both have their beginnings in the events that happened here. The founder of the religion called Islam is also believed to have made a journey to the capital city, Jerusalem. As a result of all this, the area is often referred to as 'the Holy Land' and Jerusalem as 'the Holy City'.

▼ Christianity
Jerusalem is an important place for Christians—the place where Jesus was put to death, buried and (so Jesus' followers claim) rose to life again. A church has been built on the site where some believe he was buried. Here, Christian pilgrims queue to enter the little room built above the supposed tomb.

▲ Islam
The golden dome in this picture belongs to a very special building in Islam. It is the Dome of the Rock, a mosque in Jerusalem built on the place where, it is claimed, Abraham planned to sacrifice his son. (The story of Abraham is in the Bible and the Qur'an, the special book of Islam.)

▲ Judaism
Jerusalem is also a special place for Jews—the capital of the land where, long ago, their ancestors made their home and the place where they built a temple to God. The ancient wall in this picture is all that remains of the last temple, the one built by Herod the Great.

A typical scene
Rolling hills cut into terraced fields and dotted with shrubs that can survive the long, hot summers. Throughout the settled periods of Bible times, the landscape in much of central Israel would have looked like this.

2 The Tigris and Euphrates

The northern and eastern parts of the Middle East's fertile crescent are watered by two great rivers: the Tigris and the Euphrates. The soil is rich, and people have farmed the land there for thousands of years.

The rivers are fed by the snow that falls on high mountains far away to the north-west. If falls are especially heavy, or if the thaw is sudden, the land between the rivers can suffer disastrous floods.

Ancient stories

The stories that come at the beginning of the Bible seem to be set in the region of the Tigris and the Euphrates. A creation story in the Bible says that the first people, Adam and Eve, lived in a garden paradise watered by a great river—a place called the Garden of Eden.

Another story is about a great flood. It is one of several flood stories from the area, and archaeologists have discovered evidence of several great floods.

The story of the tower of Babel may be connected with the building of huge brick temples called ziggurats, the remains of which can still be seen.

▼ Ruined tower
The remains of an ancient temple, the 'ziggurat' at Ur.

▼ Life in the marshes
In ancient times, the people who lived in the wet land by the river used the stems of marsh plants to provide a coiled framework for a type of coracle called a guffa. Bundles of reeds were used to build their homes.

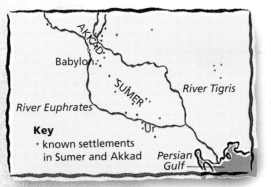

Sumer and Akkad

Around 3000 BCE the civilizations of Sumer and Akkad were established in this area. About a thousand years later, a new line of kings set up the Dynasty of Babylon. This is best remembered for its sixth king, Hammurapi, who tried to rule his people fairly with a set of 282 laws.

Assyrian Empire

By 1300 BCE, the people of Assyria to the north were growing powerful. Their empire, ruled from the capital city of Nineveh, was especially powerful from 900 BCE. They conquered many nations around them, including the people of Israel.

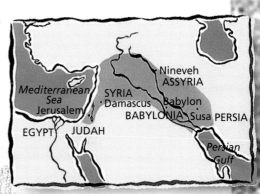

Neo-Babylonian Empire

In 612 BCE the people of Babylonia again became more powerful and beat the Assyrians. They also fought against the Israelites, and forced them to live in exile in Babylon.

Persian Empire

Persians lived to the east of Babylon. In 539 BCE their king, Cyrus, defeated Babylon and began building an even greater empire. This was finally overthrown by the Greeks, some 200 years later.

3 The Land of Egypt

The southern end of the fertile crescent curves into north Africa, and the land of Egypt. The mighty River Nile flows through this region. In ancient times, when the heavy rains fell on mountains far to the south, the river flooded its banks. The flood water spread out on the flat river plain to either side, leaving behind rich, moist soil. Here people could grow crops in abundance.

The rest of the country remained dry desert.

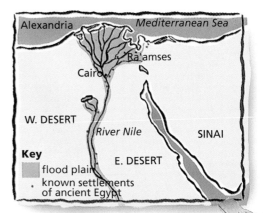

▲ **The Nile delta**
As it enters the flat land near the coast of the Mediterranean Sea, the Nile divides into many smaller rivers called distributaries. They fan out in a triangular shape called a delta.

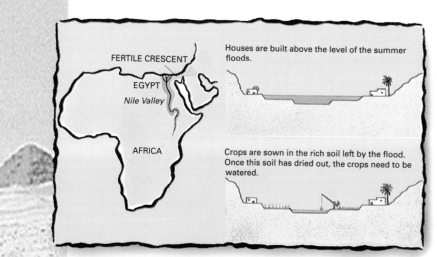

Houses are built above the level of the summer floods.

Crops are sown in the rich soil left by the flood. Once this soil has dried out, the crops need to be watered.

The yearly floods
The ancient Egyptians depended on the yearly floods to water the land so they could grow their crops. They took care to build their houses above the plain.

◀ **Farmland**
Prosperous farmland in Egypt depends on irrigation.

▼ **Desert**
Beyond the irrigated areas, Egypt is dry and barren.

▲ **A hot, dry land**
Here, rows of bricks are baked dry in the sun. Bricks have been made this way in the Middle East since ancient times. At one stage, the Israelites had to make bricks for the Egyptians.

Did you know?
Nowadays, the flow of the Nile is controlled. A dam has been built in the south at Aswan. It can contain the extra water in the flood season, and let it out over a longer period so the river does not overflow.

◄ Papyrus

In the marshes of the Nile delta grew masses of the tall papyrus sedge. Papyrus was used to make baskets and ropes. Huge bundles of papyrus were used to make canoe-shaped boats for travelling up and down the Nile.

▲ Gathering bundles of papyrus.

Here, the stalks of papyrus are being cut and bound so they can be taken to a worker who strips off the outer green skin. The inner white pith is sliced into strips, which are then pressed together to make 'sheets' of papyrus. Throughout Bible times, people wrote on papyrus with rush or reed pens and ink.

Good and bad harvests

The regular floods made Egypt prosperous. However, if the floods did not come, there would be a serious famine. The Bible tells the story of Joseph, an Israelite who rose to a position of great importance because he predicted a seven year famine and advised the king on the need to store food in advance.

Irrigating the land

Very little rain falls in Egypt, so the fertile flood plain needed to be watered during the growing season. Here, a gardener uses a shadoof—a pole with a weight on one end that can be used as a simple crane. The empty container was lowered into the water and filled. Then the weight on the shadoof helped lift it up and the pole was swung round so the water could be emptied into irrigation ditches.

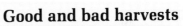

4 The Land of Israel

The Old Testament tells the story of the nation of Israel. After years of wandering, followed by years in Egypt where they became slaves, the Bible says that God brought the people to the land of Canaan. Here they were to make their home.

The 'land of Israel' shown here does not reflect the borders of present-day Israel. It simply shows the land where the people of Israel made their home thousands of years ago, and where many of the events of the Bible took place.

▼ Pilgrims
A family group from the time of Jesus have travelled by foot and donkey to be in Jerusalem for a religious festival.

▼ Hills and valleys
This map shows where the main hills, valleys and plains are found. You can read more about them in this book.

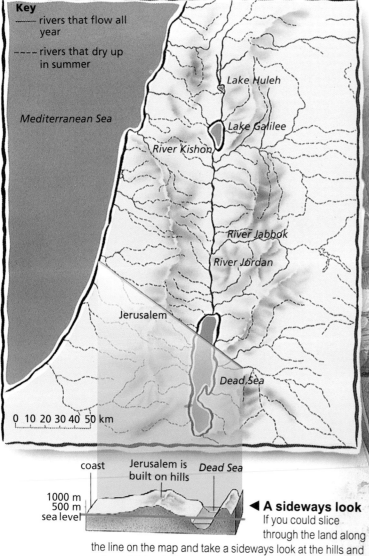

Key
—— rivers that flow all
year

---- rivers that dry up
in summer

Mediterranean Sea

Lake Huleh

Lake Galilee

River Kishon

River Jabbok

River Jordan

Jerusalem

Dead Sea

0 10 20 30 40 50 km

coast | Jerusalem is | Dead Sea
built on hills

1000 m
500 m
sea level

◀ A sideways look
If you could slice through the land along the line on the map and take a sideways look at the hills and valleys, this is what you would see. The mountains are not very high, but the Dead Sea is very low—the lowest place on earth.

A small country

The region shown on the map is quite small: around 280 kilometres from north to south, and 160 kilometres from east to west. Many trade routes passed through the region, linking the great empires to the north and to the south.

Throughout Bible times, it was fairly easy to travel by foot from one region to another. Even ordinary people might travel on occasion—perhaps to celebrate a religious festival in a special place. From the time when Solomon built a temple in Jerusalem, many people made the effort to travel there. In Jesus' day, people from his home village of Nazareth near Lake Galilee would go there as a group each year.

5 Seasons of the Year

The land of Israel has several different types of climate. The hotter, drier climates are found in the low valleys and towards the south. The hills to the north have a cooler, wetter climate.

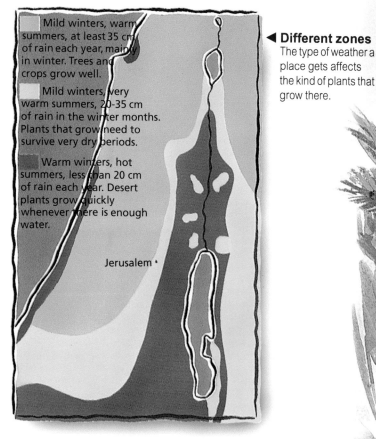

Mild winters, warm summers, at least 35 cm of rain each year, mainly in winter. Trees and crops grow well.

Mild winters, very warm summers, 20-35 cm of rain in the winter months. Plants that grow need to survive very dry periods.

Warm winters, hot summers, less than 20 cm of rain each year. Desert plants grow quickly whenever there is enough water.

Jerusalem •

◀ **Different zones**
The type of weather a place gets affects the kind of plants that grow there.

Winter

A large part of the land of Israel has mild winters. The first rainfall of the season—what some Bible translations call the 'former rains'—can be expected in October. Heavy rain comes in November. Stream beds that are dry at other times of the year fill up, and sudden downpours can cause floods severe enough to block roads. However, these floods do not last very long.

The temperature falls. There may even be frost on the hills. Snow is rare except on the mountains, but every 10 or 20 years snow falls in hill-top Jerusalem, and even on the low land.

However, it is mild enough for autumn-sown crops to grow, and the countryside is green.

Spring

As soon as the temperature rises in March, the crops and wild flowers grow rapidly, and the countryside is bright with colourful flowers. The weather is showery: these are the 'later rains' referred to in some translations of the Bible.

It is getting warmer, but some days are still chilly. On other days, a hot, dry wind full of desert dust blows from the south.

This is the time of year when birds such as storks and eagles migrate from Africa to Europe. People can often see them flying overhead.

▶**Harvest fruits**
The rich colours of the autumn grape harvest.

Summer and autumn

Little or no rain falls after April—the long, hot days of summer have started. The plants that grow wild turn brown, and the grain crops that were sown just before winter are soon ready for harvesting. Fruits such as pomegranates, figs and grapes ripen in succession. Several religious festivals celebrate different events in the farming year.

6 In the Wilderness

A huge desert area stretches from the River Tigris across Arabia and the Jordan to the Negev and Sinai—and beyond to Egypt and the Sahara.

You can even see an area of desert from Jerusalem: the Judean desert is not far away, and it reaches north for some distance up the Jordan Valley, and south alongside the Dead Sea.

Some areas of the desert are flat and stony. Other parts are sandy, with dunes that shift and change in the wind. The mountains of the Negev have rocks and cliffs.

▲ **Desert landscapes**
Desert landscapes around Israel

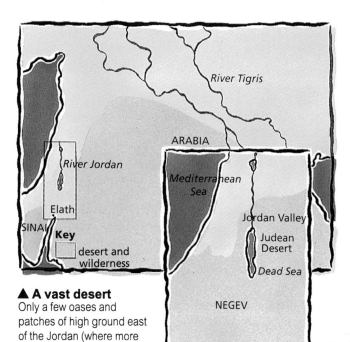

▲ **A vast desert**
Only a few oases and patches of high ground east of the Jordan (where more rain falls) interrupt this vast desert.

Did you know?
After rain, seeds in the rocks and sand germinate very quickly in a hot desert, and soon the ground is covered with flowers.

Escape to the desert
The desert has often provided a place of escape. In Bible times bandits might lurk there, waiting for a lonely traveller to attack. A wanted man might hide there—as the young David did when Saul turned against him. Jesus spent forty days alone in the Judean wilderness just before he began his work of teaching and preaching.

▶ **Desert travelers**
Throughout Bible times traders with their strings of pack animals—caravans—carried goods for sale across the desert as they made their way to the places where people lived. From Bible times to the present, nomadic peoples have lived in tents in the desert, moving as necessary to find grazing for their flocks of sheep and goats and for their camels.

Animals of the desert

The kinds of animals that would have roamed the desert wild in Bible times can still be seen in a sanctuary at Hai Bar, north of Elath.

Viper
The horned viper is a deadly snake of the desert.

Gazelle
A type of gazelle is native to the desert. It never drinks water—instead, it obtains the fluid it needs from the sparse vegetation it eats.

Onager
The onager is similar to the wild ass that used to roam the region feeding on the tough desert grasses.

Oryx
The desert oryx has a white coat that reflects back some of the heat of the desert sun.

Rock hyrax
The rock hyrax lives among the cliffs.

7 Along the Coast

All along the coast is an area of low land. Ancient trade routes from Egypt to Syria mainly kept close to the coast, where the modern cities of Gaza, Ashdod and Tel Aviv are today.

Further inland was dense oak forest and impenetrable swamp.

Ports

The waves of the Mediterranean Sea pound the smooth coastline, and there are few safe anchorages.

Jaffa, or Joppa, was one of the few places where rocks provided natural protection to harbour boats. It is now part of the sprawling city of Tel Aviv. To Jaffa came rafts of cedar trunks, floated in this way down from Lebanon before being hauled up to Jerusalem for Solomon's temple.

Further north is the port of Caesarea. There was already a port here when, in 13 BCE, King Herod the Great set about rebuilding the town and improving the harbour.

◄ **The coastal lands**

▲ **Oak forest**
These oak-covered slopes are a reminder of how the land looked in Bible times. Nowadays on the plains there are orange orchards in place of oaks. Elsewhere, low-lying swamps have been drained to provide land for farms and towns.

Mountains by the sea

The Carmel range of mountains, of which Mount Carmel itself is the highest peak, overlooks the Mediterranean Sea. On the limestone cliffs at the western end of Mount Carmel, the prophet Elijah and his servant saw a 'cloud no bigger than a man's hand'—the first sign of change in the weather, a great storm that ended a severe drought.

▼ Mount Carmel

▼ **Battle plain**
A view from the fort of Megiddo to the plain beyond. Several great battles of the Bible were fought on the plain of Megiddo. The last book of the Bible, Revelation, speaks of a great battle at the end of time, which will take place at a great battle site. For the writer of Revelation, this could only be at the 'mountain of Megiddo'—Har Magedon or Armageddon.

Megiddo

For thousands of years the city of Megiddo has guarded the road in the pass over the Carmel Range of mountains that takes the traveller from the coast on to the Vale of Esdraelon.

Megiddo was built by the Canaanites, though it was captured by the Egyptians, and held by them for centuries. King Solomon of Israel made it one of his great fortified cities and a base for his cavalry.

The ruins of his city and the huge well that provided a water supply can still be seen.

8 The Source of the Jordan

◀ **Mount Hermon**
The snows on Mount Hermon
feed the River Jordan.

On a clear day you can stand on the shore of Lake Galilee and blink at the gleaming snow on Mount Hermon, to the north. The water in the lake, and in the River Jordan that both feeds and drains the lake, has come from the melted snow. This water gushes out at the foot of Mount Hermon at Dan and Caesarea Philippi—present-day Baniyas. This is the source of the Jordan.

▲ **The north of the country**

◀ **Jordan springs at Dan**
Silvery water gushes out of the rock at Dan, one of the sources of the Jordan. When the Israelites settled the land of Canaan, the tribe of Dan captured the Phoenician city of Laish and renamed it Dan. It became a byword for 'the most northerly point in the land'. 'From Dan to Beersheba' meant the whole country, from Dan in the north to Beersheba in the south.

Unfortunately for the inhabitants, it was open to attack from the north and was eventually reduced to just a village.

Caesarea Philippi

The spring at Caesarea Philippi gushes out with silvery spray throughout the year. All around is lush greenery. In ancient times, the people who lived in the region thought it must be a place of the gods. Niches were cut in the rock and idols placed in them. In Roman times it was a place to worship the god Pan, and there was also a shrine to the Emperor.

▲ **Hazor**
Hazor was an important Canaanite city when Joshua led the settlement of the land. Its king, Jabin, tried to resist the Israelites, but failed. Later, Hazor became one of Solomon's fortified cities, like Megiddo and Gezer. It was eventually conquered by the Assyrians, in 732 BCE.

▼ **Huleh marshes**
Part of the Huleh marshes have been set aside as a nature reserve, with papyrus swamps and areas of open water.

Huleh Valley

Between the region of Caesarea Philippi and Lake Galilee is a 'rift valley', formed where part of the earth's surface has cracked and slipped down. The waters of the Jordan spread out on this flat land and once formed a large area of marshland, the Huleh marshes. Since the 1950s these have been mostly drained to provide farm land with fishponds in between.

Galilee is best known in the Bible as the region where Jesus spent most of his life. Part of the region is mountain: in Bible times, not many people lived there. In the lower hills were a few towns and villages, such as Nazareth. Many towns bordered Lake Galilee and the people who lived in them were mainly busy with farming or fishing.

▼ A busy road

In Bible times, the main route between Egypt and Damascus passed by the shores of Lake Galilee.

In this scene from the time of Jesus, rumbling waggons loaded with fish, fruit and vegetables for market jostle with marching soldiers and long distance travellers. The Roman soldier has the right to ask anyone to carry his pack one Roman mile—something which many people resent doing.

Also on the road are pilgrims travelling north to the pagan shrines at Caesarea Philippi. Other people with various ailments are travelling south, hoping for a cure when they bathe in the hot, salt springs at Tiberias on the western side of the lake.

▼ Places in Galilee

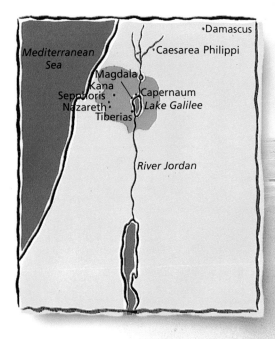

Map showing: Mediterranean Sea, Damascus, Caesarea Philippi, Magdala, Kana, Sepphoris, Nazareth, Capernaum, Lake Galilee, Tiberias, River Jordan

Did you know?

In Jesus' day, Galilee was the kind of place people sneered at and made jokes about. One young man, Nathanael, found it hard to believe that Jesus could be an important person simply because of where he came from. 'Can anything good come out of Nazareth?' he joked to his brother. The religious leaders firmly believed that no prophet could ever come out of Galilee.

Towns by the lake

In Jesus' day there were many little villages around the lake. Most of these no longer exist, but those that do give us a glimpse of the kind of places Jesus would have known. In some, ruins of buildings from the time of Jesus have been discovered.

Tiberias was a Roman city, founded in in 20 CE by the local ruler, Herod Antipas. He named it after the Roman emperor. It was a non-Jewish town, famed for its hot springs nearby. Today it is the busiest town of the region, and a centre for the many tourists who come to rediscover the places where Jesus lived.

Magdala is a fishing village on the western shore. One of Jesus' closest friends probably came from Magdala. She is known as Mary Magdalene in the Bible—one of the people who went back to Jesus' tomb. She is the woman who mistook the risen Jesus for the gardener.

Capernaum is the town where Jesus' disciple, Peter, lived. Jesus himself made it his home base after he was rejected by the people in Nazareth. It was a busy fishing town, with a large synagogue.

Towns in the hills

Nazareth is surrounded by hills with thin, boulder-strewn soil that in places gives way to bare, rocky cliffs. Today it is a busy market town. It is the place where Jesus grew up and learned the same trade as Joseph—a builder and carpenter.

To the north of Nazareth lies the village of Kana. This may be the place called Cana in the Bible stories of Jesus. Jesus was invited to a wedding in Cana, and when the host ran out of wine, Jesus turned water into more wine.

In the time of Jesus, the ruler of Galilee, Herod Antipas, built the city of Sepphoris in the hills of Galilee.

10 Farming in Galilee

Galilee is a region of hills. Wild boar can still be found in the woodland, and in spring the slopes are ablaze with flowers.

Farming has long been an important occupation in this region, and the hillsides have been cut into terraced fields.

▲ Flowers of Galilee
In spring the hillsides are a riot of colour.

▲ Terraced fields
In the hills of Galilee small patches of soil on rocky terraces are used for fruit trees or cereal crops. The stones were cleared by hand and put in heaps or used for terrace walls, which help stop the soil being washed down the hill in the rain. The red soil is fertile in places where it is moist and deep enough for the roots of plants.

▲ Shepherds
Young shepherds with both sheep and goats in the hills of Galilee in New Testament times.

▲ Sheepfold
A sheepfold wall topped with thorns protects
the sheep from wild animals at night.

Looking after flocks

Where the soil was poor—as on the higher hills of Galilee—
shepherds could still find grazing for their flocks. Shepherds
would lead their sheep to a good grazing area, and the sheep
would follow their shepherd's call. During the day, the
shepherd would keep the sheep safe from straying and
getting stuck in dangerous places, and would also drive off
any wild animals with a stone from a slingshot or by
brandishing a club.

At night, the sheep would be led into a stone-walled
sheepfold. Thorn branches laid around the top helped stop
wild animals climbing in to raid the flock, and the shepherd
would lie across the entrance to stop sheep escaping and keep
them safe.

▲ Sheep
Sheep graze in a rock-strewn pasture

11 Fishing on Lake Galilee

Lake Galilee is a large freshwater lake about 21 km long and 11 km wide. It is situated in a deep valley, and is in fact 206 metres below sea level. Sudden winds blow across the lake from the hills to the east and west, causing violent storms.

Jesus chose several of his disciples from among the people who fished for a living on Lake Galilee. Some fish were sold locally. Others were salted or dried to stop them going bad so they could be sold in more distant places.

▼ A typical view
Lake Galilee and the hills beyond often are bathed in a mauve light.

▼ Boat mosaic
This mosaic picture of a sailing boat was found in a pavement at the lakeside town of Magdala. It dates from Roman times.

Fishing boats

Fishing was done from small wooden boats. In 1985, when the level of the lake fell to unusually low levels, a fishing boat from New Testament times was found sunken in Lake Galilee. It was 8.2 metres long by 2.35 metres wide, made from planks of cedar. The inside 'ribs' were made of oak. It was an open rowing boat, and it may have had a mast for a sail.

Did you know?

Lake Galilee is sometimes referred to in the Bible as the Sea of Chinnereth or Lake Gennesaret. Nowadays it is called Lake Kineret. These three names all come from a Hebrew word meaning 'harp', which refers to its shape.

▼ Fish of the lake

About 25 types of fish are caught in Lake Galilee. One type is the Tilapia, often called St Peter's fish—a large fish rather like a carp, and very good eating!

▼ A cast net

Throwing a circular cast net.

▲ Harbours

Lake Galilee does not have any natural harbours. In Jesus' day, people used large fieldstones and boulders to build breakwaters, jetties and quaysides. Here, fishermen would sit to mend their nets after they had landed their catch.

At Magdala, the remains of a breakwater 60 metres wide and 70 metres wide still survive.

Fishing nets

Sometimes fish were caught on hooks on a line or speared, but the more usual method was to fish with a net made of linen string. A circular cast net was thrown out into the water; a dragnet was pulled through the water from the side of a boat. These nets must have been quite large—the New Testament tells of a large catch of 153 fish.

Nets tear easily, and need to be mended frequently.

12 Along the River Jordan

The River Jordan flows through a deep valley between Lake Galilee and the Dead Sea. This valley is 105 kilometres long, and all of it is well below sea level. Millions of years ago, earthquakes caused that piece of land to drop, creating a strip of low ground called a rift valley, with steep mountains either side. This rift valley actually continues for thousands of kilometres south of the Dead Sea.

Once, this area was actually under the sea. As a result, the land was worn level.

►**The Jordan**
A stretch of the Jordan with forest on each bank.

Wilderness and farmland

In a hot, dry summer the Jordan Valley is a dusty wilderness. However, the soil is very fertile, and the places that are watered by streams flowing down the hills into the Jordan can produce crops. Because it is below sea level, the valley gets very hot and the farms can produce crops of fruit and vegetables earlier than in cooler parts of the country.

However, the water near the Dead Sea gets saltier and saltier—and so does the land. The saltiness makes the land by the shore useless for farming.

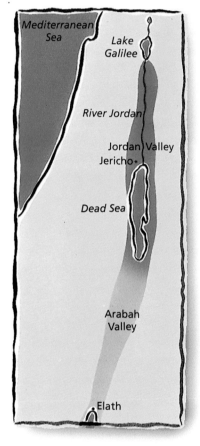

▲ **The Jordan valley region**

 Did you know?
Small earthquakes still occur in the Jordan Valley.

◄ **Jericho**
Jericho lies in the deep valley through which the Jordan flows, at a point where the valley floor widens to a plain. There has been a town here for thousands of years: natural springs make the place an oasis, and crops can be grown easily.

Forest

The Jordan meanders through a flat valley, and along its banks is a forest of tamarisk and poplar trees. In Bible times this riverside jungle was even thicker and was a place where wild animals lurked and reared their young.

Forest animals

Some of the animals that used to roam the forest by the Jordan have now disappeared from the region. These include the lion, leopard, bear and wolf. Others, such as the wild boar, gazelle and jackal, have become less common.

▼ **When lions roamed the forest**

Lion
The Bible often mentions lions. They hid among the trees of the Jordan Valley and hunted on the open hillsides on either side. As a shepherd boy, David had killed lions and bears that threatened his sheep on the hills near Bethlehem.

The last lions in this region were killed eight or nine hundred years ago.

Leopard
The leopard is a secretive creature which hides among trees and rocks waiting to prey on wild gazelles or a flock of goats. Leopards were shot on sight by local hunters, for their beautifully spotted coat was much prized. There are few left in the region.

Syrian bear
The species of brown bears that lived in this region had paler fur than European brown bears. Bears used to be common animals in the hills and sometimes took refuge in the forest. They are now extinct in the region.

Wolf
Until quite recently wolves were always a threat to flocks and shepherds had to guard their animals day and night. Wolves still live in the desert country of the Negev.

Hippopotamus
It seems likely that hippopotami used to live in the Jordan Valley. They would have wallowed in the river all day, and at night come to feed on the plants on the banks of the river. The book of Job in the Bible talks about a creature called the *behemoth* and many translators think this word refers to the hippopotamus.

13 The Dead Sea

The Dead Sea is the lowest place anywhere on earth—an amazing 393 metres below sea level. In places the dramatic slopes of the Judean Desert rise straight up from the waterside. There is little space even for the one road on the western shore that allows travellers to pass this way. A new road has recently been constructed with difficulty on the east side.

▲ Salt cliffs
A layer of salt gives an eerie effect to the cliffs around the Dead Sea.

Where nothing lives

The water of the River Jordan flows into the Dead Sea from the north. A number of smaller rivers also flow into it. But then the water is trapped: there is no outlet from this low-lying pit.

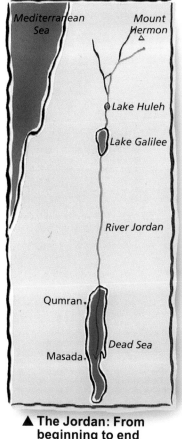

▲ The Jordan: From beginning to end

However, the water can evaporate, and does so quite quickly in the intense heat—up to 43°C in summer. The water vapour that rises up leaves behind the salt the water contained. This process has gone on for thousands of years, with the result that the amount of salt in water from the Dead Sea is five times that found in the same amount of water from the Mediterranean.

Salt

At the shallow south end of the Dead Sea the salt is so thick it is white like ice. Anything that floats there, such as a stick, is quickly coated in salt, like hoar frost.

Nowadays, the salt is collected from the bottom of shallow pools after they have dried up. They are then flooded with more Dead Sea water, which is in turn allowed to evaporate and the salt is left behind.

Pillars of salt

There are many tall columns of rock salt along the road beside the Dead Sea. These are often linked to the Bible story about Abraham's nephew, Lot, and his family. They were living in a town in this region called Sodom. The people who lived in Sodom and the neighbouring town of Gomorrah did many wicked things. Eventually, the towns were destroyed: it seems there was an earthquake and a fire. Lot and his family escaped—but Lot's wife stopped to look back, and was overwhelmed in the rain of salt. In the story, it says she was turned into a 'pillar of salt'.

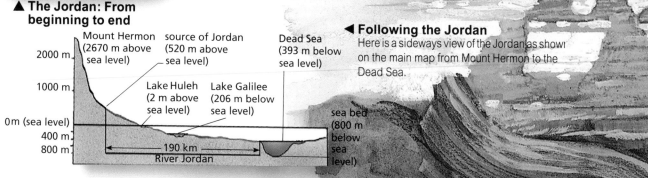

◄ Following the Jordan
Here is a sideways view of the Jordan as shown on the main map from Mount Hermon to the Dead Sea.

▲ Qumran

In the desert area around Qumran, ancient copies of parts of the Bible have been found. They have been remarkably preserved in the dry desert conditions.

▲ Masada

Overlooking the south-western corner of the Dead Sea is the hill of Masada. This flat-topped hill was turned into a fortress by the Jewish kings who ruled about 100 years before Jesus. Herod the Great strengthened it and used it as a palace in the winter time and a place of escape in time of trouble.

About 30 years after the time of Jesus, there was fighting between the Jews and the Romans who ruled them. Jerusalem was destroyed. About 1,000 Jews fled to Masada and defied the Roman army which besieged them. Eventually, the Romans built a huge earth ramp that would enable them to reach the top of the hill. The Jews committed suicide rather than face defeat and torture.

Did you know?

The amount of salt in the Dead Sea stops things sinking as quickly as they do in less salty water. People who try to swim in it find it hard going—the body simply floats on the surface. But bathers must be careful not to let the water splash into their eyes!

▼ A parched land

Travellers must bring their own water to quench their thirst when they are by the Dead Sea. The heat is intense, but the shimmering sea water is too salty to drink.

14 The Highlands

A great hump of highland runs from the north of the land of Israel to the south: from Mount Carmel and Jezreel down to Hebron and beyond. The hills extend for a short way into the Negev desert.

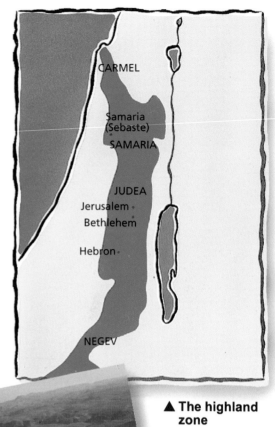

▲ The highland zone

East and West

What a difference there is between the western and eastern sides of this highland! In winter, rain falls on the western side where trees, shrubs and wild flowers flourish as well as crops. But just over the top of the hills down the eastern side is parched land, and beyond, glaring white desert, without trees or crops.

▲ A western side landscape

◄ An eastern side landscape

The western slopes

In Bible times, the slopes were covered in woodland of oaks, terebinths, Judas trees and strawberry trees. There are still nature reserves where this woodland can be seen.

Today, some of the region has been planted with pines. In other places, the land has been terraced to provide fields for olive trees and grape vines.

In places where the natural woodland has been cut for centuries, different plants flourish. Rock roses with bright, five-petalled flowers and a useless, thorny plant called spiny burnet spread their roots across the rocky areas.

Where there is shallow soil, wild flowers such as anemones, tulips and the white star-of-Bethlehem are brilliant in springtime. In the springtime, a range of plants provide grazing for herds of sheep and goats, but most dry up and wither in the hot summer sun.

▲ Woodland
The natural woodland consists of dense thickets.

Samaria

The town of Samaria, also called Sebaste, gives its name to the northern area of highland. Samaria was founded about 880 BCE by a king named Omri. Years had passed since the time of Solomon and the land of Israel was divided into the kingdom of Judah in the south, where Jerusalem was, and Israel in the north. Omri built the city of Samaria to be the capital of his northern kingdom. Omri's son, King Ahab, had a palace here lavishly decorated with ivory.

The centre of ancient Israel

Along the top of the highland is more level ground where Jerusalem and other important cities were built. This was the centre of ancient Israel where the tribes of Manasseh, Ephraim, Benjamin and Judah had settled. Later the southern part became known as Judea and the northern part as Samaria.

◀ **Picking olives**
Olive trees live for hundreds of years and grow a thick, hollow trunk. But they are never very tall—only about the size of an apple tree.

The traditional way to harvest the crop was to beat the branches so the green or black fruits fell to the ground. The olives were then crushed to extract the oil.

◀ **Grapevines**
The deeper soil found on terraced fields allows people to grow grapevines for their juicy grapes.

◀ **Wild flowers**
In spring bright flowers grow among the rocks.

15 Jerusalem City

Ancient Jerusalem was a small town on a steep hill, a natural fortress perched on the highlands of Canaan at 811 metres. The barren Judean desert to the east and the steep valleys from the coastal plain up the western side of the highland helped to defend the city. But an enemy could easily approach along the high plateau from the north or south.

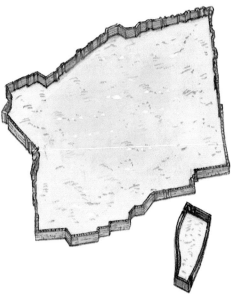

▼ The modern city
Jerusalem today spreads over several hills and valleys. The golden dome of a mosque now occupies the site of earlier Jewish temples.

▲ David's city
When the people of Israel settled Canaan during the time of Joshua, some places remained in the hands of the Canaanites. One of these was the walled city of Jebus. David, Israel's second king, chose this place to be his capital city.

To capture the fort, it seems that he and his men hacked a way into the tunnel that linked the spring of Gihon outside the walls to the city.

Hebron

Hebron is a town thirty kilometres south of Jerusalem (see page 14). David made it the capital city of his kingdom for seven years—before he captured the Canaanite city he renamed Jerusalem.

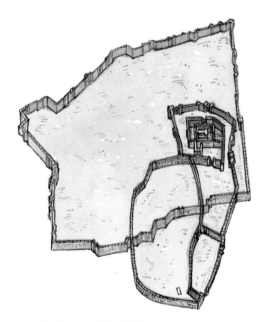

Key to diagram

The blue walls shown on the diagrams are the ones you would see today if you went to old Jerusalem. They were built many years after the Bible times. The brown walls are those of Bible times.

▲ Solomon's building programme

Solomon extended the city walls to the north, to protect some new and magnificent buildings, including a royal palace and a splendid temple.

After Solomon, it seems the city was built out to the west. However, although the city prospered for a couple of centuries, it was captured by the Babylonian army and Solomon's temple was destroyed.

▲ The Jerusalem of Jesus' day

By the time of Jesus, the Jews had been able to rebuild their capital city. The shape of Jerusalem was the result of great building schemes carried out by King Herod the Great. He had ordered the construction of the new temple that stood on the site of Solomon's temple and the one that had been built to replace it in later centuries.

◀ In the part of Jerusalem called the Upper City was Herod's palace. The Roman governors after Herod lived here and this would have been where Jesus was brought before the governor Pontius Pilate.

▼ At the north-west corner of the temple courtyard was the strong Fort of Antonia, where Roman troops were garrisoned.

Much of the Jerusalem of Jesus' day was destroyed by the Romans when the Jews revolted against them in 70 CE.

16 Places Around Jerusalem

Several of the most famous places of the Bible are found in the area around Jerusalem.

▲ **Garden of Gethsemane**
Across the brook Kidron that flows round Jerusalem is the Garden of Gethsemane—the place where Jesus was betrayed by Judas and arrested. It is an olive grove.

▲ **Mount of Olives**
From Gethsemane, a diagonal path up the hillside leads to the top of Olivet, the Mount of Olives. The Bible says that when Jesus visited Jerusalem for the last time, he stood here and wept for Jerusalem, which lay before him.

▲ **Bethlehem**
Bethlehem lies just 9 kilometres south of Jerusalem. The rolling hills between the two places is today almost entirely built up. Bethlehem is best known as the birthplace of Jesus. This church has been built around the cave where, according to tradition, the birth actually took place.

► **Bethany**
On the eastern slopes of the Mount of Olives lies the village of Bethany, made famous as the home of some special friends of Jesus: Mary, Martha, and their brother Lazarus. The Bible says that Lazarus died, but Jesus brought him back to life.

17 East of the Jordan

Green fields at the north end, barren desert to the south—these are the hills to the east of the Jordan, the 'trans-Jordan'. They rise steeply away from the long valley where the Jordan flows.

▲ Fertile hills of Bashan

The beauty of Gilead

To the south of Bashan lies the land of Gilead, separated from Bashan by the River Yarmuq, which flows into the Jordan. Gilead is higher than Bashan, much of it over 1000 metres, and snowy in winter. The natural woodland has, in some places, been cleared to make room for olive trees and vines.

It was in Gilead that the people of Israel assembled before crossing the Jordan to Jericho. Later, the tribes of Reuben and Gad settled there.

Another river, the Jabbok, flows from these hills to the Jordan. In its valley Jacob made his peace with his brother Esau.

Bashan

The hills to the north catch the winter rainfall making them green and wooded. These are the Golan Heights—Bashan of the Bible—with a wide plateau on top where the land is farmed for wheat.

However, the dry, stony desert is never far away and the great flat plains that extend eastwards are dry and barren.

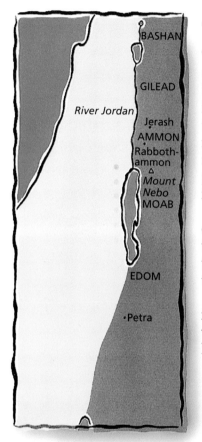

BASHAN
GILEAD
River Jordan
Jerash
AMMON
Rabboth-
ammon
Mount
Nebo
MOAB
EDOM
Petra

▲ **The 'trans-Jordan' regions east of the Jordan**
The Old Testament often mentions the peoples who lived in these areas, and the disputes that sprung up between them and the people of Israel.

▶**Jerash**
In the time of Jesus, the Gilead region was referred to as the Decapolis—a region with ten Greek towns. One of them is Jerash, sometimes called Gerasa.

A mysterious city in Edom

Edom means red—and this region takes its name from the red rock. Hidden among the red cliffs lies the mysterious city of Petra. Carved in the rock cliffs are beautiful temples and tombs dating from the time of the Greek empire. Here lived people called the Nabateans, who controlled the routes from southern Arabia and charged the traders a tax to use them.

▲ **Petra in Edom**
Buildings are carved into the rock itself.

◀ **Moses' glimpse of the future**
Moses led the Israelites to Canaan where he believed God would give them a prosperous future. But Moses himself only glimpsed the land from east of the Jordan. From there, he might have seen the Jericho oasis and the hills beyond.

Ammon—east of the Dead Sea

Highland continues south of Gilead into Ammon. The present-day city Amman, capital of Jordan, was known as Rabboth-ammon in the Bible and is the place where the great prophet Elisha anointed Jehu as king of Israel.
Later it became the Greek city of Philadelphia, one of the towns of the so-called Decapolis.

Along the highland lay the ancient trade route called the King's Highway. The people of Israel finally approached the land of Canaan where they were to make their home along this route. When they reached Mount Nebo, their leader, Moses, looked across to the land they were to settle. However, he died without reaching it.

18 Syria and Asia Minor

To the north of Israel lies Syria. Much of Syria is desert, but winter rain from the Mediterranean Sea waters its coastlands and makes them good for growing crops. This region is part of the Middle East's great fertile crescent. Throughout Bible times it was criss-crossed with routes that linked the civilizations of the north with that of Egypt in the south.

Further north is Asia Minor, known today as Turkey. The eastern part of this region is highland and snow-topped mountains—among them the Ararat range where, according to story, Noah's ark came to rest. To the west are rolling lowlands which are good for farming.

▼ **A varied landscape**
Mountains and rolling plains of Asia Minor.

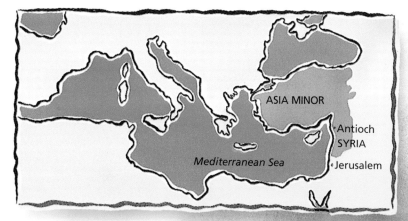

▼ **Hittite soldiers**
Iron weapons enabled the Hittite army to control a large empire in ancient times.

Hittites

The ancient people of Syria and Asia Minor were the Hittites. Their civilization belongs to the later Bronze Age: it flourished from around the time of Abraham (1800 BCE) to that of Moses (1200 BCE). Around 1350 BCE the Hittites discovered how to smelt iron successfully. This made them world leaders in technology—and marked the beginning of the widespread use of iron: the Iron Age.

▲ The theatre at Ephesus
One of the first Christians, Paul, caused a riot when he brought the news of Jesus to Ephesus. He and his friends were at the mercy of the mob at this Roman theatre.

The first Christians

When the Hittite empire crumbled this region, including the land of Israel, became part of other mighty empires: first the Assyrian empire, then the Babylonian, Persian and Greek. It became very wealthy, and many beautiful cities with fine buildings in the Greek style were set up.

In New Testament times, when Romans ruled all the lands of the Mediterranean, Christians came to this region with their message about Jesus. The Bible book of Acts tells about their journeyings and particularly about the work of Paul, who was a native of Tarsus in Asia Minor. Many of the first churches—groups of Christians—were established in this region.

▼ Roman temple
The remains of this Roman temple to the Emperor Hadrian are also at Ephesus. Evidence of the time when Romans ruled a huge empire can be found throughout the region.

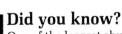

Did you know?
One of the largest churches of New Testament times was at Antioch in Syria. It was here that the followers of Jesus were first called 'Christians'.

19 Macedonia and Greece

The Greek peninsular juts out into the eastern Mediterranean. The southern part is mountainous and some of the mountains form offshore islands.

Very little land can be used for farming. From ancient times the Greeks had to find other ways to obtain what they needed. They became great traders, travelling the seas in large ships—such as triremes with three sets of oars.

About three hundred years before the time of Jesus, a Greek leader who became called Alexander the Great built a huge empire that spread far to the east.

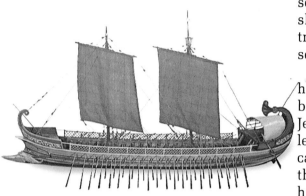

▲ An ancient Greek warship

The Greek city known as Athens became a very important centre for culture, with fine temples and places where great thinkers met to discuss ideas with each other and with their students.

At the same time, Corinth became an important port, carrying trade between the Aegean Sea and the Adriatic Sea.

▼ **Christianity for the Greeks in Athens**
One of the first Christians, Paul, was bold in taking the news about Jesus to non-Jewish people. At Athens, with its many temples, he took the message of Christianity to people with a completely different religious background.

MACEDONIA

Athens

GREECE

Mediterranean Sea

•Jerusalem

▲ **The Greek peninsula**
The Greek peninsula provided the bridge by which Christianity reached Europe from the Middle East.

Island people

In ancient times, the peoples of the islands to the south of Greece became rich and powerful. The people were experienced sailors, bringing trade to the lands on the Mediterranean shore. For this reason they became known on the mainland as the 'Sea People'. The Philistines—enemies of the people of Israel from the time of Joshua to that of David—are the best known of these. From their name comes one of the names of the land—'Palestine'.

▶ A typical Greek landscape

Macedonia

Ancient Macedonia was a separate country north of Greece. Its rolling plains are good for farming. Its forested hills provided timber, and underground lay precious metals that could be mined.

One of the great milestones in the history of Christianity happened when the message of Jesus was brought by Paul to Macedonia. Paul believed that God was telling him to take the message to all people, no matter what their background.

20 Italy

In ancient times, the mountainous peninsular known today as Italy was densely wooded. However, the lower slopes of the hills and the areas of rolling plain made good farmland, watered by the winter rains. In the region emerged the most powerful of all the ancient civilization: that of Rome.

It grew from a city state on seven hills to a mighty empire which took over from that of the Greeks and extended across Europe.

▲ **The Italian peninsula is easy to recognise**

▲ **An Italian landscape**
The vineyards and olive groves of Italy make a landscape like that of Israel itself.

▲ Colosseum

The colosseum in Rome was where cruel and dangerous sports were staged for public entertainment. Trained fighters called gladiators fought wild animals such as lions or each other—often to the death. Prisoners were executed in horrific ways before large crowds. Among these were Christians, thrown to hungry lions to be killed and eaten as prey.

▲ Forum

Today visitors can still see streets and buildings from ancient Rome. There were beautiful monuments, public buildings and private homes called villas built from the wealth the Romans made when they conquered other lands and made the people pay taxes. The forum or market had shops and stalls where Romans could buy luxuries imported from other countries in the Empire.

◄ Catacombs

Christians were forbidden to meet together in Rome in the early years of Christianity. They met secretly in underground burial tunnels known as the catacombs. The fish was a secret symbol they used, and it can be seen marked on the walls.

Finding Out More

If you want to know more about what you've read in *Where the World Began*, you can look up the stories in the Bible.

The usual shorthand method has been used to refer to Bible passages. Each Bible book is split into chapters and verses. Take **Deuteronomy 32:48–49**, for example. This refers to Deuteronomy; chapter 32; verses 48–49.

1   Lands of the Bible

Deuteronomy 32:48–49	**Lands of the Bible**
Genesis 37:26–28; Exodus 3:7–8; *Jeremiah 1:13–15*	**The 'fertile crescent'**
Acts 17:16–17, 28:16; *Revelation 2:8–11*	**The lands of the Mediterranean**
Genesis 22:1–18	**Islam**
2 Samuel 5:6–12, 1 Kings 6:1–38, *Ezra 3:7—6:18*	**Judaism**
Matthew 27:32, Mark 15:21—16:7, *Luke 23:26—24:12,* *John 19:17—20:10*	**Christianity**

2   The Tigris and Euphrates

Genesis 2:10–14; 6:9—9:17; *11:1–9*	**Ancient stories**
Exodus 1:22—2:10	**Life in the marshes**
2 Kings 17:5–6	**Assyrian Empire**
Daniel 1:1–3	**Neo Babylonian Empire**
Daniel 1:21	**Persian Empire**

3   The Land of Egypt

Exodus 15:22	**Desert**
Exodus 5:6–19	**A hot, dry land**
Exodus 7:14–25	**The yearly floods**
Genesis 41:1–57	**Good and bad harvests**

4   The Land of Israel

1 Kings 6:1–38, Luke 2:41–42 **A small country**	

5   Seasons of the Year

Deuteronomy 28:11–12, *Proverbs 26:1*	**Winter**
Jeremiah 8:7, *Matthew 6:28–30*	**Spring**
John 15:1–4	**Harvest Fruits**
Leviticus 23:9–43	**Summer and autumn**

6   In the Wilderness

1 Samuel 23:14, Matthew 4:1–11, *Mark 1:12–13, Luke 4:1–13*	**Escape to the desert**
Judges 15:14–16	**Onager**
Song of Songs 2:9	**Gazelle**
Isaiah 11:8	**Viper**
Genesis 13:1–12; 37:25	**Desert travellers**

7   Along the Coast

1 Kings 5:8–9, *Acts 9:36–43; 10:1–33*	**Ports**
1 Kings 18:41–45	**Mountains by the sea**
Revelation 16:14	**Battle plain**
1 Kings 4:12	**Megiddo**

8   The Source of the Jordan

Psalm 133	**Mount Hermon**
Joshua 19:40–48	**Jordan springs at Dan**
Matthew 16:13-16	**A special place**
Joshua 11:1–11	**Hazor**

Index